Which
Way Was
North

poems

Which Way Was North

ANNE PIERSON WIESE

Louisiana State University Press

Baton Rouge

Published by Louisiana State University Press
lsupress.org

LSU Press Paperback Original

DESIGNER: Mandy McDonald Scallan
TYPEFACE: Whitman, text; Qualion, display

Cover photograph courtesy of the author.

Library of Congress Cataloging-in-Publication Data

Names: Wiese, Anne Pierson, author.
Title: Which way was North : poems / Anne Pierson Wiese.
Description: Baton Rouge : Louisiana State University Press, [2023]
Identifiers: LCCN 2022062102 (print) | LCCN 2022062103 (ebook) | ISBN
    978-0-8071-7931-4 (paperback) | ISBN 978-0-8071-8074-7 (pdf) | ISBN
    978-0-8071-8073-0 (epub)
Subjects: LCGFT: Poetry.
Classification: LCC PS3623.I385 W54 2023 (print) | LCC PS3623.I385
    (ebook) | DDC 811/.6—dc23/eng/20230109
LC record available at https://lccn.loc.gov/2022062102
LC ebook record available at https://lccn.loc.gov/2022062103

CONTENTS

II. BAYSIDE, QUEENS, AS SEEN FROM THE WINDOW OF A CAR

ACKNOWLEDGMENTS

The poems in this collection have appeared in a variety of journals, to the editors of which I am grateful. I would also like to thank the Trustees under the will of Amy Lowell and the South Dakota Arts Council for their valuable support, along with my parents, Jim and Gail Wiese, and Dorothy James, for being part of it. Finally, and always—for Ben Miller, my love.

American Literary Review: "The Obstructed View"; *Antioch Review:* "Peeling Apples"; *Atlanta Review:* "This Is the Century"; *Bateau:* "The Path"; *Bellevue Literary Review:* "Bones"; *The Bridport Prize Anthology:* "Wild Turkey"; *Gargoyle:* "Bird on Barck Street" and "Out of Reach"; *Hanging Loose:* "Dangling Bell," "Sharp Shadows," and "Welcome, Stranger"; *The Hopkins Review:* "Doves Drying" and "Beyond the Blue Ring"; *The Hudson Review:* "Wild Grapes," "Ice Machine," "Out Front," "A Deepness in Myself Where Seasons Live," "The Cats of 148th Street," and "Red Bird"; *Image:* "Some Saint"; *Literary Imagination:* "I've Seen Graveyards"; *The Malahat Review:* "Goddamn Man" and "Late Tomato"; *Mantis:* "Autocorrect for Beauty"; *The New England Review:* "I Keep Dialing" and "In Praise of Paper"; *Ploughshares:* "Inscrutable Twist," "Middle Distance," and "Thinking About Moss"; *Prairie Schooner:* "Fort Dodge Calcium Products"; *Raritan:* "Harvest," "Making Beauty," "Macy's Supra," "The Rest of Human History," "In the Sculpture Garden," "Curtains Change," and "Hotel St. George"; *The South Carolina Review:* "Airport Sparrow" and "The Unharmed"; *Southern Humanities Review:* "Subway Preacher"; *Southern Poetry Review:* "It," "Bias Cut," "Family Recipe," "Corn," and "Due North"; *The Southern Review:* "Sutliff Bridge," "Lincoln Elementary School," "Bayside, Queens, as Seen from the Window of a Car," and "Cambridge Self Storage"; *Southwest Review:* "Life In a House In the Upper Midwest," "Sleep Is the Journey," and "The Writer"; and *The Virginia Quarterly Review:* "The Radio Tells Us It's Snowing in Montauk."

Which Way Was North

Inscrutable Twist

The twist of the stream was inscrutable.
It was a seemingly run-of-the-mill
stream that flowed for several miles by the side
of Route 302 in northern Vermont—
and presumably does still—but I've not
been back there for what seems like a long time.

I have it in my mind's eye, the way
one crested a rise and rounded a corner
on the narrow blacktop, going west, and saw
off to the left in the flat green meadow
the stream turning briefly back on itself
to form a perfect loop—a useless light-filled
water noose or fragment of moon's cursive,
a sign or message of some kind—but left behind.

I. LIFE IN A HOUSE IN THE UPPER MIDWEST

Autocorrect for Beauty

Leaving work one afternoon, I saw a hawk
on the pergola in the formal garden where
no one ever goes. We thought we needed beauty—
and we do—but humans often screw things up.

The hawk stood watching and waiting, bright
tail burning sumac red in the vacant white
and brown of winter. I knew he'd outlast
me—zero degrees as it was—but still
I stayed, watching him watch.

I've passed the empty pergola at least five
hundred times since then, in every kind
of weather, but if I look, my hawk is there:
beauty by surprise overrides all succeeding
days—and so the part of us that isn't us survives.

Dangling Bell

After winter's white submarine night star-
fished with crows stroking wind-thick space,
we came up in stages—like spring bulbs
and deep-sea divers—blind, smelling
light and stretching for it with wobbly
necks and chins raised at the sun.

Birds with colored feathers suddenly
were in the yard—coral and gem-winged,
swimming on the pendulum feeder,
tropical fish on the chicken-wire fence.

From inside our human bell, we watched
as sea and sky became the same—
our slight and separate sins released
to float up like finger bones from shipwreck.

Life in a House in the Upper Midwest

After winter, the surge of our green yard.
Din of birds morning, noon, and night.
Grass growing again in naked gulps.
The sky steeps the sun until 10 p.m.
In the fire pit, hot coals open their mouths
like baby birds—city of red gullets.

Kevin comes to clean the boiler.
He explains that most boiler malfunctions
are due not to mechanical but human
failure. This boiler sucks in air. We
know fire needs oxygen and matter
to live. Look at all the dust and dryer
lint and otherwise foreign particles
you've got down here. Not to be gross,
but that sweet smell in the fall is your
dead skin cells burning off. He places
his hand on the big blue machine:
if we weren't around, she'd work forever.

We cannot help shedding our mortal bits
in windy gusts like the quaking aspen
in the yard, but we are more like Judy's
evergreen next door—seeming green
year round until one year we are brown.
We are not seasonal. We do not harbor
and regenerate. We burn until we die.

Doves Drying

I didn't know doves could look like machine
parts. They were out there early, after rain,
on the crushed red rocks in the fire pit,
elevating one wing, then the other,
at angles suggesting breakage—sheered
flywheel blades, bent feather rotors, hidden
breasts two disks of dawn, a pair of them, like
always, together wet, together drying.

At first, I thought the strong wind
overnight had blown in metal scraps
from the street work down the block.
Then I saw injured birds and thought
how will I finish them off? But they
were whole, methodically exposing
their flight gear to the new air,
tendons warming luxuriously.

Doves, anvils of melancholy, there is hope
when such invisible weight can fly.

It

The salt tossing, crack leaping, lucky rabbit's
foot keeping part of us—the part that wakes
in the night knowing this weightlessness
is dangerous—craves a final destination,
as if not having one makes the rest meaningless.

A plain headstone in a graveyard is what you
picture: a bench, a beat-up watering can, dapple,
the fleeting overlap of green paths left in the grass
by the mower, in winter the cuddle of blown snow
wrapping each stone in a cowl of elegant obscurity.

This is the child learning death who never
leaves us and who, in charge of nothing,
seeks something true—a lilac bush—*ollie
ollie oxen free*—a pair of granite wings.

Sutliff Bridge

You wouldn't know about the bridge, bar and store
unless you were local, but now that the flood
waters are down, everyone is coming to stand
and stare at the empty space: half a bridge gone,
grabbed in the river's fist, twisted and dragged
downstream to where its dark skeletal tips break
the gentle surface, pointing awry at the sky
like rusty hindsight exclamations of distress.

People murmur that the lost half should be brought back.
It could be retrieved, restored—just a matter
of allocating the money and equipment.
But will the county ante up? It was an old
bridge with scabrous cement piers, wooden planks
that roared like thunder when you drove
over them, and diminutive spans shedding
flakes at every vibration—the puce metallic bits
freckling the roadway until the wind blew
them away. There's a newer bridge upstream—
it survived this flood and looks good for a few more.

The Sutliff store used to sell everything from seeds
to paraffin to aspirin to boots. But it's been fifty
years and now the high tin-ceilinged room—with its
bounty of varnished shelves and drawers and marble
countertops, its glass display cases a remote
emphasis of emptiness and dust, its spindle
of parcel string still hanging at shoulder height
near the silent brass register—serves only as a way
to pass from the original bar to the recent dining
addition out back, so new that its exterior
still reads, Kevlar Kevlar Kevlar, from every angle.

They do a booming business in Old Milwaukee pencil-
necks, fried bluegill baskets, and chili dogs. You can
eat inside while the jukebox skips and mingles
with talk of tractor parts and DVDs, or go
out to the riverbank where a few guys
have their lines in, casting for trout or bass
around the weeds under the bridge.

Imagine, after the flood with what newly brilliantined
suddenness the sunlight must have struck through
the water where there had been the shade of the bridge
for more than a hundred years—weeds and fish shocked
in an aqueous net of umber turning to neon green,
skated upon by the movements of clouds.

Visitors in the know write their names on dollar bills
and tape them to the low ceiling and walls of the bar—
a glaze of long-forgotten singles ambered by age
and grease and smoke. The old ladies like it here,
parking their walkers along the wall, and the farmers
wanting lunch and conversation, and the Harley
riders who come through the screen door in groups
with dust from the gravel road blunting the shine
on their leather. Since the bridge went out, bar business
has been even better than usual. No one needs strong
black thread or lampwicks anymore, but they still
want potatoes piping hot out of the oil and a place
to congregate, and this small destruction—no human
deaths involved—means nature's power affirmed,
the satisfaction of fretting over an impersonal loss,
and a blank in the air that looks like change.

Fort Dodge Calcium Products

We get off the highway near Fort Dodge, looking
for a bathroom, and all the dirt is white. Gravel spits
and pops under our tires, and white dust envelops us—
I can smell it coming through the air vents. Gypsum
is manufactured here, and calcium—when it's not
Sunday. Later, our room at the guest house shows
signs of recent renovation, white paint petering
out in an awkward corner—soft cobweb shade
of drywall: who knows what's behind drywall?

Old plaster is what I grew up with: it cannot hide
its flaws or conceal the past beneath its skin.
Old plaster never lies, but cracks slowly within
time's drag, bulges with the gravity of existence—
like flesh, like now, from dust, like us, to dust.

I Keep Dialing

Let's face it: dials are out of date. Now
we initiate change with buttons or
simulacra thereof—a spot we click
on a screen to conjure one thing or another.
I know it's old hat, but I miss the in between
dials gave us, the way our fingers used to
learn a liquid touch, trying late at night
to get Chicago or New York or across-the-
border, somewhere far away from our transistor
radio sitting on a windowsill, antenna
adjusted this way and that, reception waxing
and waning with the shifting of the wind
so that the static matched the sifting
of the leaves in the trees outside. When you
have a dial, you have access to a space
that can always be divided in half,
the infinity approaching zero meaning
more degrees of difference than you'll ever
need—it's the knowing that they're there—all
the little voices in the dark you might pull in
if you twist and turn just right. Patience
always pays when it comes to dials. I can
feel them yet—the ones on the front
of my mother's Slattery gas stove circa
1949. It was still in the apartment when
we moved in, and she saved it for the burners,
old though it was and drafty for baking
cakes or roasting meats. They don't make those
anymore—not for any money—the heavy black
dials with their honeyed spin, their play delicate
enough to make flames that leap up like woozy
pinnacles and melt back to their blue-ring
hearts as slowly as dusk: the setting of control
                              that used to belong to us.

Bias Cut

My mother taught me it's all in the pins.
The rest never stuck, or rather stuck
in ways that merely irritated me—
tan, tissue-paper collar pattern-piece
clinging to my sweaty elbow as I searched
for it in the welter of unfamiliar
sewing paraphernalia on the dining
room table, those cursed inverted notches
I didn't bother to cut and as my mother
warned came back to haunt me, the lesson
of facing: do not omit what's called for,
even though no one will know it's there but you.

But I do remember how to pin—and why.
Pin firmly. Pin at small, evenly spaced
intervals. Do not stint on pins. Pin until
you prick your finger and draw blood. Pin
as if your life depends on it, because it does.

Wild Grapes

There were grape vines climbing up one end
of the clothesline in their yard—tentative
green tenterhooks with curlicue citrine
shoots no thicker than hairs floating
on the summer air. Pointedly ignored
by my grandmother, every August they
produced several diminutive clusters
of grapes the color of opals. Not fit to eat,
my grandmother said, which may or may
not have been true: she'd grown up a child
of sharecroppers and in later life was
resolute in her refusal to engage with
the dirt or anything that came out of it.

Birds were her thing: laserlike purple
martins that skimmed but never touched
the ground, electric finches in their branch
heaven, even sparrows—so modest yet
possessed of wings. My grandfather,
with his encyclopedic knowledge of cattle,
crops and roads, dwellings, weeds and lunch
counters, could probably have told me
something about the grapes, but it never
occurred to me to ask, since the clothesline—
and everything attached to it—was women's work.

By the time I knew them, my grandparents
didn't say much to each other beyond what
was unavoidable: I remember my grandfather
flipping his table knife around—holding
the blade—pointing the back end at a bowl
of butter, my grandmother passing it.

What my grandfather loved was heading
uptown to the F & M Cafe at 5 a.m. to sit
with his cronies, sip weak coffee, smoke
a pipe, converse about more ways than
one to skin a cat—jack-of-all-trades,
master of none. I was from far away,
a city where grapes from some nameless
other place accrued in slain heaps beside
the apples and bananas in the A & P.
This was before kiwi fruit came to the USA,
or cable TV—or anything digital. Back
then all the clocks still had faces.

I never ate one of the clothesline grapes—
they were so local they were off limits;
after all, I only came for summer visits,
and although I was young, I knew
the distance between tasting and living.

Family Recipe

I never met Aunt Mamie—or maybe once
when I was too young to remember, but
there was also an Aunt Manda, who died
before I was born—or was it the other way
around? Whose Never Fail Pie Crust recipe
now never fails me—Mamie's or Manda's? And
were they real aunts—or aunts by courtesy?

These days, I am haunted by moot questions.
When you're young, you don't ask—life seems
long and pie crust dull. Later on, with just a few
of us alive and cooking, we spare ourselves those
whetstone words—who and why—that only
serve to sharpen the knife of what we know:
we Always Fail in our effort not to die.

Late Tomato

It reminds me of when my cousin and I
pricked our index fingers with a sewing
needle filched from my mother's work basket.
She had come to visit, but would be leaving
soon. The blood pact was her idea. Mine
was that I would perform any act
under the sun to demonstrate my love.   .

There is an alien red drop in the bleached
and weightless tangle of tomato plants
breathing their last all week—dead, no, still
harboring some unseen trickle of green
nourishment on which this lone tomato
has flourished: smaller and brighter than all
the rest—late, and if not best, then only.

Middle Distance

In the church, midweek at noon,
there is a middle distance
between the piercing blue
window of pure belief
and the bone vault housing
my heart's disbelief, a dim
yielding distance related
to my prayer: another day's
delay before you are nowhere—
for death fixes all distances
                    like a new nail.

The Path

Again the silent magnolias'
bruised white applause breaks
over the grass—
single petals, tongues poised
like damask questions
on the path.

When I was young
I took them home
in my pockets—
but learned that hard
things travel better.

Now I let questions
lie and pick up
rocks.

Bird on Barck Street

My father was given a BB gun, like
other boys in town. On Barck Street
he took aim at a robin—for fun, to see
if he could—and brought it down.

He never used the gun again,
although it stayed around
the house while he grew up
and went away and people died.

The lost and found of life has no
premises. We're in it before we
realize, touching what we thought
was gone. Angrily my father asked,

Where did this come from?
And handed me the gun.

Beyond the Blue Ring

> The opportunity to ride a camel doesn't come to everyone.
> —excerpt from a letter written to me by my grandfather in 1968

I remember that ride.
The camel's high barnyard
smell and lashed indifferent
eye. The pity for which
I had no words. The sick
swaying when we began
to move slowly around
the perimeter of the small
blue ring set up at the Brooklyn
street fair. The boatlike list
of the double saddle in which
I sat with another little girl—
one on either side
of the bony twitchy hump
in which the camel stored
extra water for long
walks across the desert.

Even at four I could tell
that the camel keeper
with his ratty turban
and drooping whip
had no plans to travel
beyond the blue ring.

My father must have told
his father about the ride
during one of their Sunday
phone calls. The distance
between New York City
and rural Minnesota

in 1968 was one over which
an appendage filled
with spare water might well
have come in handy.

Instead there were my grandfather's
cautiously typed letters
addressed to me, tapering
off over the successive
years to my annual
birthday card with a ten
dollar bill tucked in
and the adjuration not
to spend it all in one place.

Reading the old letters
now, I see they were
composed less for me
than for my father—full
of coy advice: *Anne, don't
let your dad crowd you out
of your room with books,* or
*tell your dad it's time to get
behind* OUR *president.*

After all, at that age
and that distance I could
have been no more to him
than a small blond blank.
But I choose to believe
the line about the camel
was really meant for me—
the stranger that by then
he knew I would become.

Harvest

Clasp of grief and chafe of grain—
we're too far gone to get home again.

Wayne's dream red combine shaves
the section, gulping silver cornstalks
in its path, green grain wagon heeling
as the tandem crests the swells, visible
then hidden in the bottoms. From I-90
or the air, you can't gauge the heave
of this land—how after Becky's pulled
pork buns and pickles on the tailgate
we can take a walk and lose ourselves.

Two men in the field, plus Leon and Nic
driving the trucks to the grain elevator
in Edgerton—a skeleton crew when you
think how it used to be: gangs of hired
hands from far and near bedding down
in barns and sheds, wolfing fruit pies
and iced buttermilk in the kitchens
of the farmhouses to which they traveled
many miles during harvest time.

Under this white ocean sky wands of sun
furled with mist curve down and sizzle out
against the churn of black chemical earth
and stalk waste. From the west, a God-like
helmet of steel mildew rain approaches.
Up in the combine's climate-controlled cab
behind tinted glass, a pink skull gazes back.

Peeling Apples

Once a year, for the apple dressing,
my mother peeled apples, standing
at the kitchen counter, wicked
paring knife skimming around the fruit
in a sketchy spiral, the goal—aside
from our holiday dinner—to get the skin
off whole, a strip that when held up dangled
gently, constricted by the physics
of having been round into a hieroglyph,
red and pale with something of green
in between, a vegetable cypher that I,
with my dull knife, could never replicate—
for all the concentration I possess, I did
not have the right hands then or now to prize
a fortune out of nowhere, tossing the un-
broken peel over my left shoulder
into thin air to read in its shape
where it fell on our blistered floor
the first letter of my future husband's
name—another poor girl's game my mother
taught me that did not take: the truth is,
you lose your mother or your mother loses you.

Bones

Big leg bones
of cows sawed
into round sections
that when broiled
erupt thick burps
of marrow—hidden
elixir heated until
it turns to cream,
loses its spark,
becomes edible.

A spinal tap is when
they push a long
hollow needle into
the base of your spine
and draw out drops
of cerebrospinal fluid
one by one. *It should
look like water,*
the doctor says
from behind. *If
it comes out cloudy
that's a bad sign.*

My bones.
White calcium
rib spokes,
finger splinters,
shin swords.
*Do you see how
pale they are
on the X-ray,*
the doctor asks,
here and here?

On my aunt's farm
we talked at breakfast
of how we'd cook
marrow bones
for dinner and laughed
at ourselves for planning
another meal before
finishing the one
in front of us.
The richness of choosing
your fancy is what
leaks away at last.

*We forget
our bones
are alive.*

Out of Reach

My walk to swim at the YMCA takes
me along a road full of traffic—walking
in this small city is for weirdos and the poor.
I didn't notice the old apple tree inside
the chain link fence before the apples started
to drop—most of them into the uncut grass
around the tree, a few onto the pavement
where they smashed on impact for ants and wasps.

They looked so good to me, but my hand wouldn't
fit through the fence, or beneath it. Once, the wind
carried down an apple in my path, its bruise tender
as a rusty dime. I ate it standing there, while people
in cars stared and one guy yelled something smart.
Such secret sweetness demands feet and heart.

Lincoln Elementary School

Near where I live, a school building was knocked
down years ago—one of those solid brick
elementary schools built before World War I,
with high ceilings, tall windows, wide hallways,
and a spinning globe on a platform in every
classroom. These schools are where the soldiers
came from. By the time I moved to town, a green
grass expanse was all that was left—a whole
city block, regularly mowed. There's a mound
in the southwest quadrant where I imagine
the building used to sit, surrounded on three
sides by asphalt recreation space. But I can't
find anyone who knows if they hauled
the rubble away or buried it where it fell.

It's a good block to walk around—five times
is more than a mile—because the city of Sioux
Falls keeps the sidewalks shoveled and salted
in winter, on all four sides. People here don't
walk much anymore—not like they did when
this school was built, when families had
a Model T Ford automobile only if they were
comfortably circumstanced, and horses were
strictly for distance. People walked every day—
not in circles, like me—but to school, and friends'
houses, and the grocery store, and the barber
or hair salon. These days, I've got the block
to myself, except for a lady with a dog, and a man
who mumbles and sometimes sports a paper
crown and always has a transistor radio up
to one ear, like a seashell that is giving him
serious news. Only once did he seem inclined
to match his pigeon-toed steps to mine—he

stayed politely in the grass, so we walked
together for a while. Once, I spied a big,
gray bird standing out front of a small, brown
house with a sagging porch. The bird was
making a noise like a faraway handsaw
and glaring at a tree trunk. To me, it looked
upset. I pegged it for a female domestic turkey,
although I'd never seen one anything like that
color—like smoke or slate. Was it someone's
pet, or an escapee from a slaughterhouse truck?

For months, I kept my eye on a patch of shattered
Christmas ornament—shining purple shards
in the dead grass, slowly bleaching to violet
spatter in the tides of snow and ice, emerging
fewer and dagger silver in spring's cold sunlight.
There was also a noose made of clothesline,
fraying and not big enough for a human, I
don't think. It stayed in the gutter for a long time,
until I noticed it was gone. These are only a few
of the things I've seen on my walks—with
the general idea being that everything keeps
changing around us, from behind as well as
ahead, and what's left of consequence—if
we're lucky—is one square block of local
                          geography for each of us to tread.

Sleep Is the Journey

It's April and the robins are talking
all night, damn them, up in bud-studded
bare trees along our block, barrel chests
rusty as headlamps in the streetlights'
glare, tiny freight engines steaming
and puffing at dark crossings of branches.

The bird of my mind is trapped,
battering blinds and walls in a frenzy
to be gone. But sleep is the journey
I will not take tonight—and soon
the robins' bright pistons will flash
unthinking into flight as dawn's
machine rolls through the neighborhood,
bringing distance from death to birds and men.

I've Seen Graveyards

I've seen graveyards I wouldn't mind spending
time in. Incredible how the notion
persists—that one will somehow be able
to relish one's accommodations
in the right grave as if upgraded
on reward points to a 5-star retreat.

I'd want there to be stars visible
overhead and old shade trees for hot days.
I'd want not to be crowded nor to be
lonely—just one of a friendly group gathered
in a pleasant picnic spot. I've always loved
outdoor luncheons. And don't omit the watering can
kept on a hook by the whispering pipe that draws
cold water from the dark ground for the living.

Corn

Everyone said the motorcycle
after his eighteenth birthday
was a bad idea, that it
would be the death of him,
and in June two years later,
he couldn't muscle out of a skid.

That year, the corn was knee
high by the Fourth of July
and before we could turn
around, it was over our heads.
My aunt walked into the green
puzzle every day and screamed.

Getting into the middle
of a cornfield is not
as easy as it sounds. Rushing,
voluptuous growth has
exploded the ground underfoot
into craters and troughs.

The mature stalks and leaves
are rough enough to cut you.
The rows trap the heat,
harbor weasels and wasps.
Spiders build their glinty
webs as big as boys.

It's easy to lose your sense
of direction and hard to see
the sky once you're in deep:
screaming screaming—naked
winter months laid end to end
after the field is picked and razed.

Due North

The new gadgets were eagerly purchased
at the dealerships by old men brought up
on the land who, if blindfolded and spun around
in circles, could still say which way was north—
these black egg-shaped devices mounted
atop dashboards that showed which direction
you were going: due east, due west, or somewhere
else, the red needle shimmying in the no-man's land
of hatch marks between the four true compass points.

My grandfather was such a man, raised on a farm
and a Rock County landowner himself, in favor
of frequent drives to detect small differences
in the progress of neighbors' corn fields or to inspect
hail damage after a summer storm. He had no need
of a compass, but one year when I was young, we got
off the plane from New York City to find him tickled
with this new invention—compact, ovoid proof
that technology was advancing in the right direction.

On the way home from the airport, with me in the front
passenger seat, he made a number of unnecessary
turns to show us how it worked. Pointing a finger
he instructed: Watch it now—see? Now we're going south.
Don't that beat all? It's long been known that redundant
information, if delivered in novel form, is welcome.
But it is only recently that we have learned how
to install microchips in our cars, our phones, our pets,
the flesh of our own arms, and track ourselves
and our possessions all over the planet by satellite.
It is only now that we have invented a world that frees
us from the need to know which way is north.

Thinking back to those drives with my grandfather
along blacktops so narrow they were nearly overhung
by green light-stippled leaves of corn, and down white
gravel roads blinding as sun that gave off great ghosts
of dust as we passed, I realize that his delight was never
in the compass itself, but rather in knowing more
than the compass. He'd show me how he could beat it
again and again, taking turn after turn and calling
out east-nor'-east or south-south-west before
the needless red needle could find its way there.

II. BAYSIDE, QUEENS, AS SEEN FROM THE WINDOW OF A CAR

Making Beauty

One morning on the subway, going to work,
I sat next to a young man with a deck
of cards. He could have been any young man
in jeans and a t-shirt and sneakers,
close-cropped hair. It was as if in this city
of embellishment he wished to remain
invisible, or at least—like any magician—
to invent his moments of visibility.

But his hands gave him away. The cards
in his hands were living. He barely even
looked at them as they leaped and skimmed
and ruffled, turning up midflight one, two,
three, four aces again and again! I was
pleased for him—things were going so well—
but he was in his own world and in it
there was only room for the next shuffle.

I thought about beauty—how making it
and seeing it are lonely in different ways:
one the loneliness of being in sole command,
the other of being the only witness.

Ice Machine

Outside the bodega on the corner
of Amsterdam Avenue and 150th Street
sits an ice machine of vintage make—
a seven-foot-high metal box of clanks
and sighs, its one-hinged door anchored
with a giant padlock, its sides chill
and mumbling in the summer heat. Since
it was placed new outside these premises
and started going, the street has changed
and changed again. The store too has passed
from hand to hand over the decades, losing
its commercial edge by the look of things.

But the frozen rattling heart of the ice
machine has kept beating even while
its battle-scarred body has been prey
to the whims of passing humans at all hours
of night and day: their hoodlum kicks, their
drunken poundings, their garish efforts
at advertisement and their delight
in the starry shatter of empty
bottles against an impassive surface.

Macy's Supra

In 1976, my parents bought a new TV.
It was the Macy's department store house brand:
Macy's Supra—its innards identical to those
of a fashionable name-brand set at half
the price, whispered a friendly salesman.

It came home bright and sleek—Supra—and my folks
were tickled with the savings. Now it's 2010
and the Macy's Supra lives on. Built to last,
it has lasted, and this faithfulness in the face
of a fickle world drunk on planned obsolescence
has ensnared my parents. Even after the switch
from analogue to digital signals, with the aid
of a cable box to translate, the Macy's Supra
perseveres, broadcasting the pageantry of the winter
Olympics, while my parents, lovers and hostages
of its upright electronic soul, the way it keeps
on keepin' on, watch it every day. Time was,
we believed what we possess, both inside and out,
to be—like a penny saved—a penny earned.

In Praise of Paper

Soon, they say with a sigh of relief, we will be
a paperless society. No more mess,
no wasteful excess, those forms in triplicate
a memory, print newspapers the stuff
of history. Sure, paper was fine in its time,
but now we've got everything we need to know
online. It's all in the air somewhere.
If you choose the right button you'll find it there.

No touching, though. No front nor back nor spine,
no sensation for the hands, the lap, or the back
pocket Ace Edition riding close
as a lover or a child. No important
crinkle of a letter held briefly on its journey
to you by many people you'll never meet
but who in this untraceable way have changed
your life. No gorgeous stamps, no cream laid, no onion
skin, no graph paper, college-ruled, pink
stationery, no letter openers shaped
like all kinds of things. No pages to turn,
no covers for knowledge to rest between, no lists
of what to buy at the grocery store fluttering
unnoticed to the floor in Aisle Two to be
picked up and pondered by another shopper. No class
notes copied three times by hand and carried around
for days before the final exam. No Magna
Carta, no Dead Sea Scrolls, no doctor's note.

Don't forget: we human beings are thigmotropic
like rats—we learn by touching what we pass.

The Rest of Human History

A gray typewriter sits on its matching gray
typewriting table at the curb, electric tail
trailing across the wet sidewalk, waiting,
this old duo, for the garbage truck. There's a cold
mist today—at dawn the steam heat came up
for the first time this fall. Always, there's a smell
of soaked dust with the new heat and the cracking
twig sounds of metal pipes expanding, like waking
in the forest to hear soft steps approaching.

The typewriter and its mate have been ousted
at this late date from one of the houses along
the block, in company with a balding blue
loveseat and a goose-necked lamp—small
imperishable helmet bowed to protect
its empty eye. I imagine a dim room preserved
all these years by someone set in his ways,
or perhaps out of respect for his memory.

The rest of human history will have to be lived
without typewriters, but perhaps when we are
gone, the landfills will spawn strange jungles
in which gargantuan flowers will open, revealing
at their centers a trace: the words SHIFT and SPACE.

This Is the Century

This is the century in which we will lose
the waltz. There will be one or two more
generations who know how, who have learned
in their youth to swoop and twirl in close
two-person circles, each small circle spinning
within the larger circle of the room, the whole
revolving with the unerring glint and pace
of antique clockworks, as if for the space
of the dance one might after all command time.
Then there will be a generation of those who
remember, who can describe in uncertain terms how
it looked—or might have looked—in much the same
way as we recall the looped and serifed script
in birthday letters from great grandparents.

Then those things will be gone. What use pinking
shears when no one sews? Knowledge of how to grow
vegetables by the moon will be superfluous soon.
But if it's not one thing it's another.

Why do we so stubbornly adhere to what
is already lost? The forms and signatures
of the ages change with or without us.
Dictionaries begin to be obsolete the minute
they're printed—and you could say we
do the same. Loss is what we live on.

Yet, walking into a crowded room we still hunger
to know who's ranged with whom, who's alone
against the wall, who might answer us if we spoke,
or who even exchange a glance—wordless but absolute.

Thinking About Moss

Outside a deconsecrated church
turned nightclub on Sixth Avenue remains
a thriving patch of moss, green as spring
even in winter. Tucked along the edge
of the foundation, it renews itself
imperceptibly beneath our eyes, proof
that people and their constructions change
more quickly than plants and less
predictably. We gather and disperse
under this pretext or that, flying
our beliefs like bright kites while the string
lengthens and then snaps. Which of us could say
how long that moss has lived there, sacred
in its busyness, absolute by nature?

Even if we stop to watch, we can't see
it working. Garbage men early
in the morning bowl trash cans down
the avenue in the milky light
as if aiming for a strike. Waiters
poise for a fervent smoke at the curb
before plunging back through the front doors
of restaurants. Street sellers of all stripes
hover like peripatetic hosts
torn between showcasing their wares
and consolidating them for a quick
getaway if the cops show up. Humans—
we jangle like bells with our need to be noticed,
we ring in our towers balanced on air.

Out Front

From the sidewalk cracks
out front tiny shoots
appear, roots clinging
to some unseen soupçon
of soil, unremarked
in the grand scheme
of the city street
but here year
after year—a stubborn
minority of green.

A Deepness in Myself Where Seasons Live

Certain blocks in the city lend themselves
to weather. On Monroe Place spring is always
coming soon. What moment of transcendence
in my earliest years fixed this small street
forever in March in my mind I'll never
know—but walking it now after a late ice
storm I note with satisfaction how the frozen
drips clasped along the undersides of tree
limbs and canopies hold evening's raw pink
beginnings as blue night's crest hesitates
over the rooftops, and how the sound-shadow
of a dove's call flutters in the cold, and how
strewn on the ivy lie old rags of snow waiting
                                        to be washed.

The Cats of 148th Street

Today the temperature hit sixty degrees
and all the street cats are out. Blinking
at the sun they sit choosily on dry patches
of cement, licking winter off their feet.

They've been here through the cold months, holing
up in infrastructural crannies known only
to cats and eating who knows what, these sleek
and wary slinkers curled in disused drainpipes
and boiler room nooks, their whiskers bristling
tenderly like dowsing rods for spring.

There are always one or two missing, if you've been
keeping track—but the rest are here, fur coats intact,
tails indignantly switching at puddles, untame,
unloved, and unloving of everything but life.

Red Bird

A cardinal's *chip chip* in this glassy sun-
cleft afternoon with storms on the way makes
me pause to search the trees on Edgecombe
Avenue. When I was young my mother
loved those scarlet birds and now a brilliant
flash, a tiny crest, the falling *cheer cheer*
of their call seize me with the blank
urgency of imperfect recall. Behind the hill
thunderheads felt but not yet seen are
taking their sweet time to break. The wait
from birth to death is merciless unless
we make it matter less by seeing more
and more: red bird, green tree, rim of memory—
                                        speak to me.

The Radio Tells Us It's Snowing in Montauk

It's snowing in Montauk this morning—or so
the radio tells us—not so far as the crow
flies from where Manhattan rises on its darkness
of rock, but far in other ways: a sandy limb
of land stretching east in its fierce lace of surf
and cold circuit of sea-round stones seeming
to say go farther than I can take you—distances
are what we have imagination for.

Lying in bed in the snowless city, the sleepless
night behind, the unseen garbage trucks braking and yawning
below, the radio on low, I remember standing
on that beach long ago. There was snow then, too, soft
white glims falling out of the white sky
lining everything with light: the dead brown thickets,
the sparse and leaning pines, the motels sleeping
with their storm shutters up, their neon unplugged until spring.

It took a long time to notice the white smoke
way out on the water, fitful puffs quickly torn
across the horizon by the wind. Somewhere out
there a ship was burning—burning on the ocean
in the snow! Whom could we have told in that empty
world wrapped in the slow motion of winter?
But in the end it didn't matter because it turned out
to be whales—although we could only see their spouts.

Hard to know if seeing the creatures themselves
could be any better than what I saw: all
human things at my back until I chose
to turn around, the tide drinking the snow
and the sand lying gently beneath it, while
in my mind's eye those enormous bodies rose
and blew and sank, their warm blood racing
on its invisible journey to keep them alive.

The Obstructed View

Some days peering
through the slatted
wooden wall into
the Japanese garden
is better than being
inside and seeing it all.

Everything you know
is there from other
visits, you glimpse
in strips. A view
obstructed startles
what's hidden in you—
part calling to missing part.

In the Sculpture Garden

In the sculpture garden despite the marble
and metal, the weatherproof wire chairs placed
here by humans, it is also September.
The young sparrow beating its wings at the edge
of the reflecting pool has gotten its fledging
just in time for winter. Although it can flutter
and peck on its own, still it besieges
its parent for food, reluctant—as who is not—
to let go of a good thing, as I am
to leave this garden with its wind rushes
of triangular yellow leaves, overarching
patterns of blue light, the beech's silver
dewlapped bark and the reticence of fall
in the postures of the adults sitting
on the wire chairs holding cups of coffee
like children with Magic-8 balls—shake the black
ball, tip it up, and in the round window awash
with mysterious indigo liquid
one triangle face of an icosahedron
surfaces bearing an answer to your question:
You may rely on it, or *Better not
tell you now,* or *It is certain*—always
a favorite query was, "Will I die?"

The sparrow charges my chair with dusty
mille-feuille feathers and miniature chest pumping
as if it has just learned that this is our last
hour—the seasonal prophecy we wrestle
and our secret belief that in the teeth of nature
                                        we will be spared.

Wild Turkey

Standing on the corner of 144th Street
and Convent Avenue, looking this way
and that with an air of either bewilderment
or calculation—it's hard to tell with turkeys—
she (because even from across the street you can
see the absence of wattles) attracts no small
amount of attention: a sleek, phlegmatic
wild thing shining a thousand shades of brown
in April's leaking, run-off light—long necked
and elegant until she begins to walk
down the block with the uncertain gait
of a late-night partygoer who's lost one pump
but doesn't know it yet—she heads for Amsterdam
Avenue, pausing to touch her beak to flecks
of glint embedded in the sidewalk, her fuzz-
laced dark eyes either taking in or ignoring
all us amazed gawkers, blink after blink
after blink: people in hats on their way to church,
a man with his large dog on a quickly shortened
leash, two paramedics in their truck who decline
to radio the appropriate authorities
to rescue the imperiled bird, those cracking jokes
about Sunday dinner and those marveling
at the beauty of this strayed piece of nature,
those who've never in their lives seen a live
turkey and those who've seen so many they've lost
count—all of us stopped in our tracks, including
the guy holding a bottle of booze with one hand
and his pants up with the other, all of us
unable or unwilling to move on until the big
bird gauges the space between buildings, lowers
herself for an instant like a strong but wayward
spring, and takes off with the sound of gloved

clapping, an ungainly bundle of feathers
so out of place that her sudden departure
even more than her inexplicable presence
leaves an impossible shape in the day.

Airport Sparrow

There is a sparrow in the airport
terminal. It got in by mistake
and who knows if it will ever get
out again? But perhaps my pity
is misplaced and—far from yearning
for trees and rain—the bird considers
Jet Blue gate 19 and environs to be
a perfect world: no hawks, no cats, no wind,
no snow, when peckish there are crumbs
galore and humans always making more.

This corridor is windows from ceiling
to floor, but despite the natural light
and the uncontested food supply—
a bird should be outside to die.

Bayside, Queens, as Seen from
the Window of a Car

Now it's called Oakland Gardens, my friend who is
driving the car tells me. *But back then we called
it Bayside and* I ALWAYS *say Bayside. Only
fifty-plus years and they change the name—and then
somewhere in there they invented zip codes:
Oakland Gardens, NY 11364. You're too young
to remember before zip codes.* I am, however,
old enough to have used letters when dialing
on a rotary phone the number of my best
friend growing up in Brooklyn: UL2–6715.

There are many such lost numbers still to be seen
all over Queens. They were meticulously painted
on walls and now fade infinitely on the brick
sides of old buildings, faintly urging
passersby to avail themselves of Furnished Rooms
at Reasonable Rates, Fine Quality Paste,
Fasteners—All Sorts, Superior Furnishings
for Home & Office, Smoked Fish—Wholesale & Retail,
Sewing Machines to Suit You. *And all the men
wore hats,* my friend says. *Not just the Orthodox.*

In Queens there are no tall buildings to speak of,
so the marigold light kindling through the clouds
after the summer thunderstorm settles evenly
over everything: Technicolor swathes of blue trees
shading orange Tudor houses on tidy green
plots and shopping avenues that seem to stretch,
two-storied and motley, all the way to Jamaica Bay.
The ticket to a decent American life after the war,
my friend tells me. *That's what all the people thought.
Look—there's the house my parents finally bought.*

It wasn't a dream, just long enough ago to seem
like one: Murray Cohen from the duplex next door
erupting onto the lawn in a sleeveless undershirt,
his good trousers with the crease still in, bare feet,
suspenders flapping at his sides, howling
with emotion, dancing to the curb and back, raising
his arms as if to pull down branches, and finally
throwing himself into the grass, rolling over
and over. It was 3:58 p.m. on October 31st, 1951.
The wives and mothers of Bayside came out

to watch. He's run mad, maybe? Lost his job?
When it was explained to them that the New York
Giants had just that minute beat the Brooklyn Dodgers
for the pennant on a walk-off home run by Bobby
Thomson at the Polo Grounds, they shook their heads,
pronounced: yes, definitely mad—a grown man to behave
like this for nothing more than a baseball game?
I never saw an adult run out into the street with no
shoes before, my friend says. *And those suspenders*
flapping like weird wings. The Shot Heard Round the World

was what they called that home run. You're too young
to remember, but you've probably heard about it.
What I say to myself, but not to him is: No.
Given the right place and a dying light
I can remember anything.

Sharp Shadows

On our kitchen wall at a certain time
of year appeared what we called the sharp
shadows. A slant of western light found
its way through the brown moult of fire
escape hanging on to our Brooklyn rental
building for dear life and etched replicas
of everything in its path—each bubble
and flaw in the blue glass, the blade
of every knife on the rack, the fine
hairs standing along the back of my arm.

I can't remember which month, out of twelve,
they came, only that we were stunned fresh
every year to stumble upon such undying
perfection in our kitchen—or anywhere—
lives being dreams with the edges mostly blurred.

Curtains Change

People move in and out of the apartment
opposite mine in the building across the street
frequently, but I never see them: who, how
many, where from—except the two young children
who balanced on the windowsills one day—
five floors up and nothing below but concrete.

I only see the curtains change—sometimes sheets
or blankets, or bright, insufficient beach towels.
Sometimes at night there is the agitated blue
light of a television behind them, sometimes
not. Much as I watch I'll never know the people
who come and go so quickly—or exactly why
they do—but I see them marking their present
territory, as I've done mine: if you conceive of home
                              you manage curtains.

The Writer

People in the neighborhood called him The Writer
because he loitered on certain corners for hours
at a stretch, making notations in pocket-sized
spiral notebooks. At all times of year he wore a dark
dirty overcoat. At no time did he interact
with passersby. The rumor went that he was
a Lebanese man who, either here in Brooklyn
or back in Lebanon, had lost his wife and children
to a house fire, which had driven him mad. He was tall,
thin, and furtive. Nobody could glean what he ate
or where he slept. I thought perhaps he did neither,
having been transformed by grief into a surly
exempt essence needing nothing but an infinite
series of pages no larger than his palm
on which to record a repeating pattern of dots
and dashes—some morse of misery or misery
of remorse. One year, similar rows of dots
and dashes began to appear in fluorescent
marker on the front steps of people's houses. Anxious
homeowner conversations ensued. It was the view
of some that the spooky but benign scribbling
had become a recognizable language—
that of revenge. The Writer was marking his targets.
He would arrive in the night with gasoline
and matches to take from others what had been taken
from him. But it was no such thing. There were no fires,
no raging explanations of what it was all about,
no confirmations or translations, just the dull
simmer of his continued solitary assessment,
as if he were the last man on earth—or the first.

Some Saint

There's a church where I sit
on my lunch hour when the silence
within me cries out for its counterbalance
without—the only sounds the clinks

and clanks of old radiators working
in winter and birds nesting
up in the buttresses in spring,
the mediated mumble of traffic

and the echoing feet of those who come
like me for a reason—expressed
or only a wild guess.
I sit near a statue—some saint
with keys—from whose upraised hand drops
blank grace I swallow like a stone.

Subway Preacher

There's a lot of sin in the world today—
this is the gist of what the preacher
who has planted himself in our subway
car is saying. Whatever is not
salvation is sin. So his message
is clear to everyone. It is we
who will burn in this lake of fire
he conjures with such solemn relish.

By the way, the churches are no good
either. They are under judgment too.
Salvation has become in these final
days a strictly one-on-one encounter
with Jesus. He must tell us this. He
is here to let us know. Pressed on every
side by morning commuters who roll
their eyes and plug their ears,
the preacher delivers his news.
His fierce sonority and his wild beard,
the deep breaths he takes into his barrel
chest between phrases and the way he maintains
his balance when those around him list
precariously on the curves keep crowd
response to a minimum. For instance, no
wiseass shouts SHUT UP! And no sanctimonious
type suggests that we all have a right
to our own beliefs but not the right
to inflict them on others—especially
in an enclosed space.

I think of medieval church paintings
in rural England, some of them uncovered
and restored after as much as two or three
hundred years—deliberately or mistakenly

hidden or damaged at a time when ideas
about religion were quickly changing.
They were called Doom paintings, painted not
by famous masters, but men who traveled
the wet spring hills and frost-burned moors
with their colors on their backs, men who knew
the use of red and yellow ochre taken
from the earth, rare pigment of lapis
lazuli and copper salt for green used
sparingly to illustrate the Day of Judgment
on which the saved and the sinners
shall be separated forever.

In these paintings the sinners are often shown
already filing down off the bottom
of the scene—we all know to where and it's not
a subway station—their body language
already ghastly, mouths awry and bare
limbs akimbo. Nothing can save them now.

A painter can paint a picture to make
a living without necessarily believing
the story it tells. We know this, all of us
on this subway car going to our jobs
because it's what we do every day—tell
a story of one kind or another to ourselves
or someone else—whatever it takes
to get by. So perhaps after all his urgency
is not misplaced, the lakes of fire in his eyes
not as imaginary as we might wish
but rather reflections of what he has
glimpsed in his fever, the Doom
we enter in order to live.

The Unharmed

There are people who walk along the edge
of sidewalks always, as if forced
to the margin of any communal
path, as if the tip into oncoming
vehicular traffic were only
a matter of time and circumstance,
eyes firmly on the curb, shoulders hunched
in what might be chagrin or anger
or something harder to identify.

Thirty years later I still encounter the boy
from down the block who went bald but survived
lymphoma, and my childhood playmate who kept
his hair, but as he grew older was often found
wandering the streets wearing only his socks—

and we pass in silence. These visitations
of body or mind when they come too young
can push a person to the side for good,
the center that we imagine ourselves in
having proved illusory. Notice them: they are right.
The middle of the sidewalk is dangerous
and the unharmed stride along like gods.

Welcome, Stranger

The pink neon letters make me think
of flamingos—but they say *Cocktails.*

Inside, the noise of Amsterdam Avenue
is replaced by the noncommittal mumble
of an old air conditioner and a horse race
being called at Saratoga, riders flapping
across the TV screen like a string
of rainbow-colored pennants.

The TV at the other end of the bar
is tuned to the silent green rectangle
of a golf tournament. The regulars
pay divided attention to one or the other,
their beers ranging from amber
to citrine as the long arm of the sun
reaches through the front window to rest
briefly along the bar's age-glazed wood
with its gracious sateen lip.

As I sip my martini, more details resolve
out of the brown gloom, deep shadows
becoming empty booths, crescent pieces
of darkness along the wall curving
into striped bass glinting green, the floor
a honeycomb of hexagonal blue
and white tiles—each one the size
of an oyster cracker—riven by rivers
of cracks and the vague upheavals
of time.

Covering the back wall is a murky
mural of the Rhine Valley, complete
with castle and waterfall—the sky
a grimy, valiant blue, the forest black
and impenetrable, the restrooms incorporated
by means of an arched doorway framed
with painted stone pillars, as though by following
the call of nature one might wind up
in Mainz, circa 1932.

The bartender is underweight, his motions gentle
but incessant, a damp cloth flung
over one shoulder. He knows everyone
here except me, but opens the bar-size bag
of potato chips for me and diffidently broaches
the subject of wet versus dry martinis.

Happiness catches me under the ribs—or maybe
it's the gin—this spreading glow outside history.

Goddamn Man

He comes along 149th Street from the direction
of Broadway, chanting himself home
from some bar, usually around 9 p.m.
I always hear him before I see him—
the words of his chant are liquid
and unintelligible except for its chorus
repeated in tandem with the smacking
of his cane tip on the pavement ahead:
Goddamn goddamn goddamn goddamn goddamn.

I stand, curtain held back in one hand,
watching his approach from my fifth floor
window, noting through the darkness
and downward distance the outline of age, the coat
flapping defiantly open even in winter,
the limp and the swagger and the surprising
speed at which he travels, belting
out his song that is half truculence, half
triumph: *Goddamn goddamn goddamn goddamn.*

All the way along 149th Street he goes,
a bawdy town crier who's forgotten his script
but undaunted has simply changed the message
and gone on, steadier on some days than others,
the forward lurches of his momentum
threatening but never quite causing a spill,
his receding call audible as a rising, falling
tone distinct from the other noises of a city
at night until—in less than the space of one *goddamn*—
                                        I've lost it.

Hotel St. George

On a table outside the shoe repair shop
in the ground floor of the Hotel St. George,
several rows of worn shoes are displayed
for sale, each pair buffed and mended—
looking like so many earnest souls
transmuted by some heavenly haberdasher
who in life loved to preach: We Are Our Shoes.

One wonders about the cutoff date—
how long does the proprietor wait before
deciding that the owner of this pair
of wingtips or those good Italian pumps
will not be back to pick them up?

In the window is a sign: Not Responsible
For Items Left Over 30 Days. But these shoes
are much older than that—leather fragile
and glamorous as petals, metal eyelets,
boot laces defying age by means of wax,
tongues softly collapsed onto woeful inserts
and heels clunky as 1965. No velcro!

Due to what incident or accident
does one abandon one's shoes?

The St. George was once the fanciest hotel
in Brooklyn, with ballrooms, fine restaurants,
and a saltwater swimming pool on the top
floor. But after 1964 no one wanted to stay
overnight in Brooklyn anymore, except
those down on their luck, or mad, or drunk,
or travelers having lost their way.

Grand wallpaper festooned with flower garlands,
befogged with mold, gilt wall sconces cracked
and broken like teeth, endless corridors breathing
dismantlement, punched-out locks, swooning
drapes, shattered windows and roomfuls
of pigeons, humble ranks of porcelain faucet
handles still insisting: Hot, Cold, Waste.

What gaudy, globe-trotting ghost—accustomed
to private rail cars and brocade everywhere,
oysters on ice, Long Island Duck, and bathing
clothes—would condescend to haunt this castle
of commerce laid low? An abandonment both
explicable and not to those who stayed
and watched the decades pass like transients.

Now the hotel's being redeveloped, since Brooklyn's
coming up again. One tower is student housing,
the other luxury co-ops selling at market rate.
In the ground floor old businesses hang on until
they are replaced—a unisex hair salon, the newsstand
that never left, an all-night locksmith, a Korean
grocery with cut flowers for sale by the door.

Here, beneath the weak neon of the salvaged
hotel marquee, are queued-up dead people's shoes
that despite their bargain prices will never be worn
again. There, from under newer pavement tread thin,
stray patches of the entryway's original tiles are
resurfacing: tiny blue and white porcelain hexagons
stranded like time's cumuli, their message:

All ye who enter here seeking talismans from the past,
beware: you will find them and they will not fit.

Cambridge Self Storage

Fresh to this town, I am smitten
with everything. After many years
I'm in a new place. Sun pricks
the neighborhoods I walk through clear

to their bones—brick, eaves, gravel lit
like museum exhibits I've no fear
of touching. From where I've stopped to sit
I watch lengthening shadows appear

all around Cambridge Self Storage; it's
a neat, cream-colored compound here
at Concord and Fern—windows trimmed
blue, tidy shrubs out front, in the rear

what looks like an old-time ham
radio tower, the tall, glamorous
kind manned by a lone listener—
like me—with an ear up against the future.